CRITICAL MASS

CRITICAL MASS

by Mario Murillo

*The timeless masterpiece on the
how and why of revival*

Fresh Fire Communications
425 El Pintado Road
Danville, CA 94526

Published by Fresh Fire Communications
425 El Pintado Road, Danville, CA 94526

ISBN# 0-9654598-1-0
Printed in the United States of America

To those whose hearts are hungry for
a true move of God's Spirit in our nation

Contents

Preface

Something is going to happen, in spite of the impossible odds, in spite of the hardness of our generation. Deep down inside me where the real knowing goes on, I know something is going to happen! *A great revival!*

Let's face it! The thought of a nationwide penetration of righteousness, of a true revival, seems so unreal. We can't even remember the last time the roar of God was heard in the land. We can't remember the times in American history when mayors of major cities such as Denver and Portland proclaimed revival and closed city offices and businesses to go to churches and pray.

Maybe you are like I am. You walk around with an unearthly frustration. You know something is about to happen! You hear the cry of some wonderful, invisible event that wants to be born.

This book is about that yearning that many have to see a new act of God. I count as my dearest friends those precious few who have not given up on our generation. I love those who are not deafened by the present evil. They can still hear the resurrection voice of Jesus. They know that the Holy Spirit has not abandoned us. They know that a strategy is available. They believe there is a plan to take back what Satan has stolen.

In 1982 there came a point where I was sure my mind had failed. Within me were convulsions of truth. God had removed contentment from me. I was feeling deep birth pangs. With paralyzing clarity I saw the church and my own efforts as being of little effect. My generation was largely unchanged by all the church had said and done.

Mine was the dealing of Israel by God when He said in Haggai, "Give careful thought to your ways. You have planted much, but harvested little. You eat, but never have enough. You drink but never have your fill. You put on clothes, but are not warm. You earn wages, only to put them in a purse with holes in it." (Haggai 1: 5, 6)

The resulting journey is what made this book possible. Along the way God faithfully reduced me to a child. I waited for answers. Not only did I pray, I studied, I talked to elderly saints who were in awakenings in the past.

Time passed quickly and there never seemed enough hours in a day to continue my quest.

I was disappointed to find so little written today about revival. These kinds of books must be hated by Satan. When you walk into a religious book store, you have to dig past all the books on Christian diets, dating, and mood control to find those abandoned texts that tell us of our real purpose for existing . . . to release the glory of God on a dying world.

Even when I did find books on revival, some seemed to be wrapped up in giving only two or three answers. First, most of them told of what happened in past revivals and then some told of why they thought these revivals happened. Why doesn't somebody simply tell us what to do, I wondered. I was so frustrated at the scarcity of good revival training.

I believe church historians do us a disservice if they honor past revival without trying to inspire new ones. I wanted to scream, "That's great . . . but we need another one. Now what do we do?!" How I thank God for the nuggets of truth that faithful saints have left us. Thank God for the historians who didn't embalm past revivals in honey, but reported them accurately and then pointed the way for others to happen.

So it was, after all my searching and all my crying, that God caused my slow heart to hear His Voice. Each page you are about to read is born out of my own breaking and seeking.

Before a great awakening, there must come a rude awakening.

Before you read this book, it is essential that you face specific misconceptions and attitudes that would prevent you from receiving the revelation I call "critical mass."

Here is a list of current conditions in believers that will stop truth from penetrating:

(1) Wanting "teaching" but not *training*. At first this sounds like nit-picking but look more closely. Do we love to hear deep truth without implementing it? Many have become cassette tapeworms who wallow in what they know.

Ezekiel was told by God, "They love to hear your words but they will not do them." (Ezekiel 33:31) Training is what we need. Training is different from teaching because to train someone is to require them to perform. What we need is revival training. *The content of this book is not something for you to know, it is something for you to do.*

(2) Feeling inferior to previous generations of Christians.

Again, when revival "experts" portray a past group of saints as being a better grade of believer, they violate history and they play into a tactic of Satan.

Often I've heard preachers say that the first-century Christians "shook their world without newspapers, jets, or television." Does technology give us an advantage or make people more receptive to the gospel? Absolutely not! It is today as it was then. Only a clear work of the Spirit can open men's hearts.

Paul the Apostle would be amazed by our feelings of inferiority. He would zealously encourage us and recount how very human those book of Acts saints were. If God did it for them, He can do it for us! We, like they, can seize God's grace to overcome faults.

(3) Seeing revival as an unachievable state of bliss and perfection.

None of the past revivals was perfect. When they are pictured so idealistically, one will make the mistake of thinking they are nearly impossible to get.

Grace and mercy permeate every past awakening. Revivals are a dramatic mingling of God's mercy and the occasional bungling of His servants.

(4) Abusing end-time prophecy.

Don't get me wrong; I believe in the rapture. What I reject is a defeatist attitude that uses prophecy as a cloak of decency.

End-time corruption is a very easy excuse for a fearful church. But we must not violate scripture and fashion a doctrine in order to justify our failures. Certainly things are going to "wax worse and worse" but Jesus forever sealed the issue in Matthew 24:14 when He declared a worldwide impact of His gospel before the world would be allowed to end.

That remains our task: to shake the earth with Good News. If we use scriptures out of context to tell us it can't be done, we've lost the war before the first battle.

If we are too bent on escaping the idea of attacking, Satan will bewilder us. What a strange army! A sword in one hand and a suitcase in the other. Before we ask for revival, we must be sure that we believe it can happen.

(5) Spiritual smugness.

Whether it is professionalism in a pastor or apathy in a saint, the result is the same; if God is turned a deaf ear, He will look to someone else to finish His work.

To be smug is to be falsely content with results that are skimpy. It is not an outright rejection of God's work, it is more a mixture of a sense of exaggerated self-importance and a numbing lack of urgency.

In the church today we have made it fashionable to want revival. It is "in" to talk revival talk.

Satan has not wished to bury revival talk but, rather, he wants to congratulate us for only saying we want it. He is amused by our pompous symbolic effort to bring revival.

The devil delights in the fact of our pride. We are so pleased with our awareness of the needs for revival that it seems enough to just want it.

There is a young crop of Christians that is entirely

different from the swooning saints. These young Christians ask disturbing questions about why we always seem to want something that we never deliberately try to get.

If the church is not careful, we may be passed over in favor of this new breed of believers who don't have our religious childhood diseases.

Finally, let me ask you to read each stage of revival, understanding that they are all connected in a divine progression. Don't skip ahead but let the truth open like a flower. Adapt and change according to each step of faith.

In II Chronicles 7:14 there is a promise. We've all heard it, believed it, but probably never realized its significance. Embedded in that verse are the instructions to follow in order to remove Satan's vile talons from the throat of our nation.

Critical mass is a nuclear term. It refers to the minimum amount of radioactive material that can and will sustain a nuclear chain reaction. This book seeks out those who can and will sustain a chain reaction of glory on our nation. If you are one of those, read on.

STAGE ONE:
God seeks a core

If my people, *who are called by my name, will humble themselves and pray and seek my face and turn from their wicked ways, then will I hear from heaven and will forgive their sin and will heal their land.*

II Chronicles 7:14

You are a child of God. That means that to do anything below what you were created to do will bore you. Your supernatural origin and the legacy of triumph that makes up the Christian faith demands that you do something great with your life.

There is a spirit in the land today, a spirit that insists that the individual life is of no consequence. Everywhere we turn we are shown that our particular existence is not important, that we cannot make a difference.

Nothing could be more of a lie. You have simply to look at the last 15 years to see that only a handful of people caused incredible change. Two reporters from the *Washington Post* break a story that forces a president out of office and makes Watergate a household word. A young unknown film director named George Lucas releases a movie called *Star Wars* and a whole new era in filmmaking begins. Beyond these, we have seen the breakthroughs by individuals in medicine, technology, art, literature, and the list can go on and on. The fact is that the world we live in is shaped by a handful of people.

In recent years the Christians have felt their lack of authority and responded with new emphasis on faith and the ability to claim things from God. I was refreshed to see a renewed sense of activism in Christian doctrine but I feel that all of this authority can be wasted in believing God to provide television sets when we could make the higher claim of winning an entire generation. Why not ask for cities; why not believe for drug pushers to be removed from a slum and for a tidal wave of compassion to spread among the poor and needy?!

The tragedy is that the secular world-changers do not have the magnificent gospel of the church and yet they pursue their dreams with total abandon.

We have God's Word, we have access to His Spirit. We have the most glorious purpose of any organized group on earth, yet we cannot marshal our resources to do something great for God's glory in our time.

I sense that there is a new breed of disciple that is weary of demonstrating the muscle of the church by building huge buildings. They would prefer that we channel this into the release of God for the healing of the nations. There is nothing wrong with buildings when they are constructed to facilitate an ongoing act of God. However, if they are only monuments of prestige, the money is better spent on lives.

Let's let God tell us what our individual life is capable of producing. When He said, "If my people," He was making a timeless statement. When He judges the affairs of mankind, He looks first to see what His people are doing. Before the angels entered Sodom and Gomorrah, they went to Abraham. They first inquired of the man of God. The cities were not destroyed simply because of what was there but also because of what wasn't there: a core of God's people.

Genesis 18: 24–32:

v. 24 "What if there are fifty righteous people in the city? Will you really sweep it away and not spare the place for the sake of the fifty righteous people in it?

v. 25 "Far be it from you to do such a thing—to kill the righteous with the wicked, treating the righteous and the wicked alike. Far be it from you! Will not the Judge of all the earth do right?"

v. 26 The Lord said, "If I find fifty righteous people in the city of Sodom, I will spare the whole place for their sake."

v. 27 Then Abraham spoke up again: "Now that I have been so bold as to speak to the Lord, though I am nothing but dust and ashes,

v. 28 "What if the number of the righteous is five less than fifty? Will you destroy the whole city because of five people?" "If I find forty-five there," he said, "I will not destroy it."

v. 29 Once again he spoke to him, "What if only forty are found there?" He said, "For the sake of forty, I will not do it."

v. 30 Then he said, "May the Lord not be angry, but let me speak. What if only thirty can be found there?" He answered, "I will not do it if I find thirty there."

v. 31 Abraham said, "Now that I have been so bold as

to speak to the Lord, what if only twenty can be found there?" He answered, "For the sake of twenty, I will not destroy it."

v. 32 Then he said, "May the Lord not be angry, but let me speak just once more. What if only ten can be found there?" He answered, "For the sake of ten, I will not destroy it."

It is no wonder that Satan has made it a top priority to make our existence seem futile. The fate of the nations rests in the hands of the righteous. When the beloved of God turn to Him, it has more impact than the evil that surrounds us.

God's decision to spare a nation is based upon finding and purifying His people. The depravity of our country should not preoccupy our thinking. Let's quit worrying about what they are doing and, instead, correct what we are doing.

The very first stage of revival is to establish a core. Every city needs a group that will set itself aside as a living sacrifice. These are those who want to identify themselves in God's presence as being totally available to be brought to critical mass. These people aren't rebels; they aren't out for personal glory. They do not want to split churches or walk around with superior countenances. They simply care; they only want revival.

Jesus' voice thunders across the centuries, "If any two of you shall agree as touching anything ... " (Matthew 18:19 KJV) The promise is that it will be done! It can literally start with only two. They need no great talent except to totally agree on what needs to happen.

There is no prayer that can be prayed that will bring dread upon Lucifer like our prayer made into a revival core. A revival core with the conviction, "God is going to give us this city!" The road ahead is fraught with many battles and only the truly persistent will survive. We are asking to become the literal altar upon which the fire will fall. You are enlisting in the service of God's retribution on satanic activity in your community.

Right from the start God must baptize us in His confidence and we must never take our eyes off of the righteousness of Jesus Christ. We are wrapped in it by faith and when Satan tries his usual tactic of telling us how dirty we are, we can silence him with that righteousness.

Each time God ordains a new leader, He begins by infusing him with confidence. He does not give a shallow self-confidence but a granite sense of reliance on the depth of God's commitment to Him. The burning bush meant to Moses that he would stand in Pharoah's court with the Name of God Almighty as his defense. Samuel was a living legend. When he came to the house of Jesse in search of a king, no one knew of any king. Nobody saw the raw material of greatness that lived in the scrawny boy named David. Years later David would face the brutal Saul, holding on to the memory of being ordained by Samuel. The entire book of Psalms was born from repeated triumph of David's confidence in the call of God. He faced a mountain of sorrow and thundered back from Psalm 20, "Now I know that the Lord saves his anointed!!!" (Psalm 20:6)

This confidence is not transferred nor inherited. It is personally given by God to each generation. Although Joshua had the greatest of teachers in Moses, he had to hear those words that would carry him to the finish

line, "As I was with Moses, so will I be with you."
(Joshua 1:5)

No amount of fortitude or tenacity will cover for the
feeling of being a second-class citizen. To evict devils
and establish justice, we must know beyond knowing
that our ordination to see revival is from the highest
court. How else will we come boldly to the holiest place
to plead for the cause of an entire nation?

The hordes of hell must not say to us, "Paul I know
and Jesus I know, but who are you?" (Acts 19:15) A revival core presents itself to God and waits for the man-
tle of authority with which to proceed with the strategy
of power.

Habakkuk personifies the prayer of the revival core
when he prays, "Lord, I have heard of your mighty acts
and I stand in awe of them. Renew them in our day; in
our time make them known; in wrath remember mercy."
(Habakkuk 3:2) You are entering a solemn covenant
with God to know Him as heroes of faith have known
Him in days past. But remember, He sought you before
you came to Him. There is in our God an intense desire
to find His revival core. "The eyes of the Lord range
throughout the earth to strengthen those whose heart is
fully committed to Him." (II Chronicles 16:9) He seeks
to find in us that spark that He can transform into a life
that can change the course of history.

So what is it that He looks for? The element of des-
peration to do something about the way things are. In
the book of I Samuel, we find yet another example of
this. Jonathan faced a hopeless situation: the vast army
of Philistines. Israel possessed no military might against
so large a foe. Internal strife had reduced God's army

to pitiful factions that literally hid in the holes and rocks in the surrounding countryside. Jonathan has a sudden flash of remembrance, "We are the people of God! We have a history of miraculous comebacks. Our God reigns!" Jonathan and his armor bearer became a revival core.

Listen to the words of Jonathan, "Let us go over to the outpost of those uncircumcised fellows. Nothing can hinder the Lord from saving, whether by many or by few!" (I Samuel 14:6)

And God granted a great victory to Israel that day. Rule number one is that the group exists to bring revival, that each one is there for that one reason. The home prayer gathering must undergo a revolution. Away with the cookies and coffee get-together! In other parts of the world, powerful churches meet in homes to pray. We have copied their method but we have missed their attitude. They do battle in prayer while we tend to "hang out." They seem to get things done while our "get blessed" atmosphere produces nothing. From God's perspective, the contrast is depressing. While some home prayer groups are a place of tremendous power, others degenerate into a social rumor mill. A revival core exists to meet God and receive power.

Ideally the leaders of the Body of Christ would be the first to form a revival core. However, there is a disheartening attitude in too much of our present leadership. It surfaces as a fear of allowing the Holy Spirit to be released on the congregation. Spurgeon once prayed that a divine disorder would come. More often than we care to admit, that disorder would be perceived as a threat even if it did come from God. Some charismatic leaders criticize high church ritual and yet would defend their human programs even in the face of a God-ordered suspension of those programs.

A pastor must see that if he is truly a man of God, revival is a fulfillment of all his dreams. To oppose revival is to spite everything he entered the ministry for. This is not to say that all pastors are unwilling to lead revival. In fact, I see willing pastors everywhere; that is why I know that a powerful revival is coming.

When the heart of God turns to a city, the pastor should be the first to respond. The local church is the perfect place for revival. God is intensely loyal to the local congregation and He will strive to bring them into His awakening with tremendous patience and mercy. However, the local pastor and his flock must not abuse God's loyalty to them. After repeated attempts and numerous warnings, the Spirit of God will bypass a church and its leader. We must face this because the hour has come when the urgency to stop Satan in our land must take priority over religious politics. When God puts out a call to touch a city, He will bear long but not forever with reluctant saints. Revival will be brought by another source.

The phrase "if my people" proves that choice has a part in revival. Woe unto those who say that if God wanted to move in our nation He would just do it. The blood of a whole generation is on our hands if we walk away and pretend that the evil isn't there or that God doesn't want to use us. We are the ones He is looking at, not the blind helpless masses. We possess the responsibility and the privilege of displaying His everlasting love yet once more to a dying world.

Stage one of revival is where we find our identity. "If my people" means that the people who are God's possession have been identified. Identity is the real issue in forming a revival core. The fact of our being children of God is our supreme confidence . . . not only in facing battle but also in facing God. Identity tells us what and who we are.

Identity is more important than self-esteem because our identity is the real truth about ourselves. Today we are taught to look into the mirror and say beautiful things about ourselves. Well, I looked into the mirror and, frankly, what I saw in my soul scared me to death. I could have lied to myself and steamed up self-esteem; but that won't hold up in battle or in God's presence. An honest dose of personal insight can cause despair because our nature is a cavernous well of lust, greed, and violence. It wasn't until I looked away to God and gave Him final say about my identity that real hope took hold.

Our Father will declare us as His children; He will acknowledge our needs. But with the revelation of our desperate state will come His total commitment to change us. Our tumorous inner person is dealt with in the surgical safety of His loving presence. Give me one moment alone with God where He speaks forgiveness, confidence, and identity, and I'll gladly trade it for a million catchy phrases and theories about feeling better about myself. Far more than self-esteem, we need God's esteem.

Years ago, the confidence of the church eroded. Formalism replaced dynamism. Intimidated by modern thought, many of our pulpits abandoned the counsel of

God and started passing off a lethal mixture of human philosophy and misquoted scriptures. Satan advanced and the church retreated. The once triumphant army bent on attack was diluted to a quivering club of survivalists. The church simply didn't know who she was because she had strayed from the One who could give her identity.

Once a frightened man was threshing wheat in a wine vat (that's like practicing your golf shots in a closet). God sent an angel to inspire him to action. The angel shouted, "The Lord is with you, mighty man of valor." (Judges 6:12) With all the vigor of a soufflé rising, Gideon responded, "If the Lord is with us, then why has all of this befallen us?" (Judges 6:13) The Midianites had ravaged Israel and had sent them all into hiding, but now God was trying to bring them out. The poor angel must have thought that it had gone to the wrong wine vat.

The angel was not affirming Gideon; he was identifying Gideon. Gideon thought, "I'm no hero. I'm no man of valor!" However, the angel, acting on strict orders from God, was identifying the core by which His deliverance would come to the people of Israel. Gideon was being told who he would become through God.

Our battered self-concept makes it impossible for us to imagine revival. Just wait until the valor of God replaces our timidity! Just wait until the wisdom of God replaces our programs. Just wait until He clothes us in majesty . . . terror will strike our enemy.

It all begins with that long-awaited cry, "Lord, we are your people!" As mentioned previously, the word "if" in the phrase "if my people" proves that revival is in part a matter of choice. I respect theologians who are much more learned than I but I disagree that revival is totally sovereign or that it is outside of our will to gain revival. To introduce the element of choice does not lessen God in the least. But to believe that it is completely outside of our choice to ever have revival does not glorify God. In fact, it plays into the hand of Satan by producing a passive church that senses no responsibility to its generation. God has set forth laws and principles. Each carries a blessing for obedience and a curse for disobedience. By meeting the requirements set forth for awakening, revival will come.

Perhaps the whole matter of "if my people" is summed up in the story of Isaiah. The sixth chapter of Isaiah begins with the statement, "In the year that King Uzziah died . . ." A great king had died and Isaiah feels the void and uncertainty of his generation.

It would be good here to appreciate the vast difference between the despair the prophet must have felt and the awesome power he was about to know. This will help us in this dark moment of time to have faith even though we can't imagine our generation being transformed. Isaiah felt lost and alone. The political shield of Uzziah was removed. His prayer didn't rise, it sank.

With divine irony, the thoughts of Isaiah, being thoughts of gloom and helplessness, would collide with the announcement of the seraphs, who suddenly appeared and declared, "Holy, holy, holy is the Lord God almighty. The whole earth is full of His glory!" (Isaiah 6:3) The doorposts quaked at the sound of those words! As these beings of unspeakable glory hovered overhead, Isaiah was gripped with fear. Then suddenly there was the great God Himself, high and exalted with the train of His glory filling the entire temple.

Isaiah's fear changed; at once he no longer feared the times, seasons, or conditions. He only feared the Lord!

In that pure atmosphere of glory with God in plain sight, Isaiah's whimper over his own concerns became an explosive cry. "Woe is me for I am ruined! For I am a man of unclean lips and I live among a people of unclean lips, and my eyes have seen the King, the Lord Almighty!" (Isaiah 6:5)

One of the seraphs removed a coal off the altar and touched the lips of the prophet, purging him of all that was hindering his life. He reached critical mass! God was commissioning Isaiah and with it came the powerful confidence that God always gives.

The prophet who was once afraid to leave the temple found himself eagerly awaiting instructions. God said, "Whom shall I send and who will go for us?" and Isaiah thundered back, "Here am I. Send me!" (Isaiah 6:8) That is our confidence, and that is our cry, that in the midst of a wicked people we, like Isaiah, can see the Lord high and exalted, and be sent to our time with life-bearing words.

The eyes of the Lord see everything but they focus on what is going on with His people. Let us come before Him now, aware of our total helplessness. Let us announce that we are His people and that we do not fear our time, but we fear the Lord, and we have come to stand before His presence on behalf of a new demonstration of His glory on earth.

Become that core. Find those who will join you in prayer. Now that the core is formed, let us begin our journey toward critical mass.

STAGE TWO:
The attitude that gains entrance

If my people, who are called by my name, **will humble themselves** *and pray and seek my face and turn from their wicked ways, then will I hear from heaven and will forgive their sin and will heal their land.*

II Chronicles 7:14

You have had the finger of God pointed at you. You are marked for special use.

I believe you have responded to that call or you wouldn't read on. Now we get down to business about showing God we mean it.

You are about to pray as you have never prayed before in your life. You are going to enter another world where answers come and light floods your hungry soul.

The first step has been taken; we have declared ourselves to be the chosen people of God. We have made known our intention to be set apart, to willingly depart from anything that blocks our way to power with God.

You stand before the greatest door in history. Beyond this door lie the most precious gifts of God. Beyond this door you will find the keys, the secrets of heroes of faith who have gone before you. They shook their generations, they shut the mouths of lions, they established justice and they stood, at one time, where you now stand.

Before you rap flippantly at this door, beware of the words of Jesus, "Many are called but few are chosen." (Matthew 22:14 KJV) God sends His signal to come and receive to many, but He opens the door to few. I am not speaking here of salvation but of obtaining revival.

This door is not opened by talent, persistence, nor mental prowess; it is opened by an attitude. The psalmist asked, "But who can ascend to the mountain of the Lord? but he who has clean hands and has not lifted up his soul to vanity." (Psalm 24: 3,4)

So then what is this attitude that gains entrance? Shouldn't we just pray and believe God for revival? Absolutely not! You can't instantly shake yourself from a sedentary Christian walk and casually waltz into prayer and demand a revival from a holy, awesome, all-consuming God.

To pray before uncovering our hindrances is like a priest rushing a sacrifice onto the altar of God. Not only is it futile, it can offend God.

But it is so much more than that!

When God says, "If my people who are called by My Name will humble themselves and pray . . ." it's like a loving parent at the bedside of an inebriated teenager. He is waiting for the alcohol to wear off, for the stoned child to come down off the drug.

If my people, God says, in effect, will sober up and realize what they have done and what they must now do . . .

In Luke 15:17, Jesus illustrates the return of sanity to the prodigal son. "He came to himself," Jesus says. The prodigal's attitude is precisely what I believe gains entrance to God. He realized that his father's servants were eating better than he, a full-fledged son, was eating! His temporary insanity gave way to a fiery resolve. "I'm going home," he determined. "I am willing to do anything for my father."

True humility has many vital features, the first of which is a deep realization of need. We must experience the full agony of what we have lost and what our true condition is before God.

Proverbs says that "a beautiful woman without discretion is like a pearl in the snout of a swine." (Proverbs 11:22)

America is a nation that has been baptized in blessing. She is beautiful beyond compare. Our bristling seacoasts are the world's finest; our mountains crown our nation with unequalled majesty; our rivers, valleys, forests adorn us with a splendor as no other nation on earth. Upon this glorious land God placed a people. In 1776, those New England farmers flexed, and drove a world power home to England. Not since the Jews walked through the Red Sea had a nation been born so supernaturally. A constitution followed that has become the greatest source of government in mankind's history.

Can it be possible that this great nation that crossed an ocean to stop Hitler, that opened its arms to the destitute worldwide and sent more missionaries out than any nation in history, that forged great institutions to dispense liberty and justice for all ... can it be that this priceless pearl of freedom, this jewel that once gave light to the whole world should now be in the filthy jowls of a swine?

We have believed the unthinkable lie and insane contradiction that we should save the whales while we allow over a million abortions a year. Our way of life protects criminals and ignores their victims. Marriages are shattered; the family faces extinction; teenagers take their own lives in record numbers; alcohol and cocaine are choking us to death; gonorrhea, syphilis, and the hideous newcomer, AIDS, are spreading to millions.

We have witnessed the dawn of technobarbarians, people who are reduced to savage instincts in a computer nation. They are numb from chemicals; they are ignorant of God and glued to television sets. They are the new Americans and unless God helps, they could be the last Americans. The final test of a civilization is how they treat their children and, as if to add insult to injury, unfortunate American children lucky enough to have avoided abortion will end up being molested, abused, even killed in record numbers.

I want to enrage you; I want to sicken you. I want your heartbeat to quicken, your stomach to churn, your jaw to quiver from anger and grief. I want you to see a mud-wallowing, slobbering, slime-covered swine wearing America on its snout.

Rock videos scream it, pornographers print it, movies glorify it. The message is clear. Bury the rules, put it to the limit, grab all the pleasure you can.

Innocence is beaten senseless, truths are lied about while lies are truthed about. All the while, Satan stands out back by the filth pump laughing with delight.

Whoever knocks on the door of God must pound it with the convincing force of someone who has seen the tragedy and can't bear to let it continue.

That's the first quality God looks for: someone who has been sobered, humbled to a sorrow and conviction for which there is no relief except one . . . revival.

Humility is also a determination to act. We must not arrive in the holy presence of God empty-handed.

We have come with our best. Before Him will be laid our talents, time, and priorities. To our shame, prayer has become a time to negotiate with God. There is no compromise with a king. When Paul declares that we are to present our bodies as a living sacrifice, he means to give God something that lives. This is best resolved before prayer. Paul calls this unconditional surrender our reasonable act of worship. It is totally justified and it has been reasoned out before we dare ask for audience with the King. This does not mean that we can't admit a struggle with habits or desires with our heavenly Father. Certainly we are to cast all our cares on Him because He cares for us. What we mustn't do is come defensive of our sin or thinking that God doesn't know. This is the double-minded man James described and said, "Let not that man think he will receive anything from the Lord." (James 1:6–8)

The revival person arrives saying, "I am ready."

If there is no plan to change or place for revival to go, God won't deem the prayer to be serious.

A church must consider what a citywide takeover would do before they pray for it. To pray for a river means to consider where it is going to flow.

To sit down and calculate the total consequence of spiritual awakening shows God you mean it.

Humility means knowing your place and knowing God's place. He must be treated like a king, and He insists on being approached by those who know He is able to do what is asked.

Hebrews says, "He that comes to God must believe that He is and that He is the rewarder of them that diligently seek Him." (Hebrews 11:6 KJV) That verse actually says two things about God that must be known by the person who is going to come near in prayer. Again these are pre-conditions for prayer. First, we must believe that He is! Is what? Is the "I AM" who can do mighty things. It is a recognition of His glory and omnipotence; it is, in fact, worship and intelligent praise.

The psalmist was correct in saying, "I will enter His courts with praise." (Psalm 100:4)

The second condition is to expect reward for diligence; more accurately, we must know God is a rewarder.

That is why planning for revival goes with praying for revival. If we ask for something that we can't possibly accommodate, it can only mean we didn't expect it. Expecting it means we train counselors to handle a sudden influx of new converts. It means pastors read accounts of past revivals to see potential dangers and prepare a congregation to absorb and sustain revival life.

It can even mean that meeting halls are secured and strategies for mass evangelism, including advertising, literature distribution and organized prayer, are studied carefully.

For leaders, it means something that is possibly very painful. Preparation for revival means an attitude of cooperation among leaders, a repenting of exclusivity and competition.

Some leaders will be terrified by revival when they have to face the difference between revival and "successful" church building.

Human charisma can attract a crowd, but that is not revival. A high-powered church program can bring new people but it is still not revival. There is even the reverse psychology of a laid-back approach where churches grow because they are not trying to. People are attracted by the low-key style simply because it is different, but again, this is still not revival.

There is much to be said in favor of large churches and many are powerful centers of God's Spirit. But merely because a church is large does not mean it is involved in a move of God. Even when a large church is in a move of God, it is imperative that its resources be placed at the disposal of the Holy Spirit for the next great step—a citywide impact. When leaders tell God revival is their gradual goal, they deny the urgency of the Spirit who is calling for immediate action.

I am convinced that most fears of revival are unfounded. This is no appeal for the squandering of years of work on some spooky, fanatical scheme. It is the courageous act of offering back to God His people and declaring their availability to whatever is on God's heart for the city.

Pastor Cho in Seoul, Korea, epitomizes the successful pastor who died to self and became a revival leader. As of this writing, his congregation numbers more than 500,000 people.

I believe that American pastors with congregations in the thousands don't know that revival will explode them into the tens of thousands. What we must change is our priority. Instead of large churches, let's go for strong people and release them to make a big impact upon the city.

Now we come to the final key in gaining entrance. It is

so simple and obvious that it can be overlooked. The Bible says, "If I regard iniquity in my heart, He will not hear me." (Psalm 66:18 KJV) David, while repenting in prayer, said, "Behold, you desire truth in the inward parts." (Psalm 51:6 KJV) Harbor a secret sin and you will not be heard. Jealousy, lust, bitterness, gossip, pride, name it. You must make it right prior to entering God's presence for revival.

Of course, Satan can run you in circles with guilt and condemnation, and God doesn't require that we enter His presence without weaknesses and faults. But we must not be actively practicing or harboring sin. Wherever you are convicted by the Spirit, you must make it right. Go see people, if necessary to clear the air.

As I said before, you stand before the greatest door in history. You've heard the truth; you know what will give you entrance. Go ahead, knock on it. He sees your heart. I can see it opening before you. Now we're going to do the most awesome thing we can ever do. We are going in to stand before God and ask for a true nation-transforming awakening.

STAGE THREE:
The birthing prayer

If my people, who are called by my name, will humble themselves **and pray** *and seek my face and turn from their wicked ways, then will I hear from heaven and will forgive their sin and will heal their land.*

II Chronicles 7:14

It was 3 A.M. and for no earthly reason I woke up screaming. I sat straight up in bed and could not stop the mysterious gusher of grief that was exploding from my soul.

I threw on my clothes and raced out of my house. I walked for miles, sobbing, avoiding everyone, partly because of embarrassment and partly because I wanted no one to interrupt this holy thing that was happening to me.

Fortunately, I didn't see anyone, because I must have been a grotesque sight. My body was wringing wet with perspiration and convulsions of sorrow kept coming and getting stronger and stronger.

I knew I must find a solitary place in which to pray. I sincerely believed that I was about to die from weeping.

As I stumbled along in the night, the events of the

previous week were rehearsed in my mind. The work I had founded in 1971 in Berkeley, California, was failing after two years of struggle and heartbreak. Everything we tried was thrown back into our faces. Every meeting we held in our little building was disrupted. Every day was an agony of persecution on the campus. We had no money and we were far behind in paying our staff's salaries.

But the final blows were when one of our female staff workers was attacked and when protestors threw a large rock through a window. A crib was near that window and glass landed on the six-month-old child of a couple on our staff. While the child was miraculously unharmed, the incident enraged me.

I finally took it out on God. "I quit," I said to Him . . . and that was that. I assembled the staff and told them the work would be disbanded. I went upstairs and started packing.

By about noon my Volkswagen was full of my belongings and I was going to move far away from Berkeley.

God, in His merciful timing, had me arrive at a main street of Berkeley just as thousands of students were getting out of class. They were a multitude, and my car was trapped there as they walked before me.

God arranged that trap. I was forced to sit and watch the very lost souls I was called to reach. There I was, ready to abandon them.

At some point during my two years in Berkeley, Jesus had deposited in me the love He felt for this student community. I leaned over the steering wheel and the burden and concern overwhelmed me.

I turned around and went back. I regathered my staff

and told them I was prepared to die in this city to see revival.

Those beautiful staff members made the same commitment. Whatever it was that I needed to do to hear from God, I was committed to doing it. It was not apparent to me then, but what I had done was meet God's pre-conditions for true revival prayer and intercession.

So there I was, staggering through the night desperately trying to find a place to release this torrent of prayer. Hours passed and I found a lake and buried myself in the thickest part of the trees and bushes.

To try to describe the travailing and unutterable groanings is futile. Simply believe me when I say that time stopped, my soul went behind the veil. All my life I had wanted to pray like that. I knew that heaven heard and that hell dreaded the answer that was to come.

The very place of prayer seemed to shine with God's glory. Then, as I never had heard His voice before, Jesus said to me, "The power of Satan in this city has been pierced tonight. Now you will see a breakthrough. I have given you this city."

As suddenly as the grief had come, it was gone. I felt as refreshed as if I had slept all night. I ran home and washed up, changed clothes, grabbed some gospel tracts off my dresser, and headed for Telegraph Avenue.

The campus was busy, as usual, and I felt elated that God had given me this city. I knew the frustrations of the past were gone. I zealously approached student after student, simply wanting to tell them that Jesus loved them.

Then my hope was shattered. A tall, muscular, student radical flew into a rage. "Jesus loves me, does He?

Well, I hate Him and I hate you!" he said to me. And with that, he spat in my face and tore up all my literature. A crowd was gathering to watch the preacher pay for being on campus.

Standing there alone, I felt betrayed by God and totally humiliated. This was a despair I felt sure I would not recover from. Then, without warning, a pleasant-looking young man stepped right up to the radical and confronted him gently, but firmly.

"Do you know who this young man is?" he asked. The radical, somehow knowing he should back off, calmed down and responded, "No, I don't know who he is."

"This is Mario Murillo, a man of God," the young man said. "And God has given him this city." After saying that, he cast deep, confident, knowing, loving eyes on me. Those eyes looked deep within my soul and confirmed the promise God had made to me the night before. Normally, the kind of words he used would evoke laughter from the listening students. For some reason there was a sense of respect and recognition. The radical apologized for his behavior and I told him I accepted his apology. Then I turned to find the young man but he had vanished. An angel? I have wondered for years and I still don't know. What I do know is that on that day an awakening began and within two years we had prayed with almost 2,000 young people to be born again.

My reason for telling you this incident is because revival is born out of an act we loosely refer to as prayer. However, we are in desperate need of a clearer and fuller explanation of what prayer is.

After much thought, the clearest comparison that I

could find to what I experienced is childbirth.

In revival prayer, a person presents himself before God to give birth to an act of God in his city. He is not muttering requests, he is suspending his very being between God and man. At first it is just words and petitions, but soon it envelops the person. He is reduced to one long, all-consuming declaration. His whole body becomes the prayer.

Hannah achieved this state when Eli thought she was drunk: "Hannah was praying in her heart, and her lips were moving but her voice was not heard. Eli thought she was drunk . . ." (I Samuel 1:13)

When he prayed for rain, Elijah literally assumed the position the Jewish women assumed in order to give birth. "So Ahab went off to eat and drink, but Elijah climbed to the top of Carmel, bent down to the ground and put his face between his knees." (I Kings 18:42)

The first characteristic of this kind of prayer is that it is focused. Nothing is more important for experiencing this forceful praying than to focus your concern. Tied to our lack of power in prayer is our lack of a target for our compassion.

This is the first issue. We have come to worship and pour out our deep grief over a specific evil in a specific place at a specific time.

Daniel made his point clear to God. The captivity of Jerusalem broke his heart. He exclaimed to God saying, "O Lord, listen! O Lord, forgive! O Lord, hear and act! For your sake, O my God, do not delay, because your city and your people bear your Name." (Daniel 9:19)

This is the reason Daniel prayed so effectively; he had focused his grief and love.

In Daniel 9:2, Daniel says he understood why the desolation Jeremiah had predicted had come and then he says, "So I turned to the Lord God and pleaded with him in prayer and petition, in fasting, and in sackcloth and ashes." (Daniel 9:3)

The exertion of revival prayer that gives birth is immense. That is why a person devoid of a deep heart-rending compassion for a specific city or area will not survive to see revival born.

If we aren't stunned and paralyzed by the need, our prayers can't consume us.

The second quality of this kind of prayer is that we radically change our way of knowing when to stop . . . this has frightening implications. When a woman enters a hospital to give birth, she gives up her right to a time limit. She is there to give birth. The object is to take all the time that is needed to bring forth a new life.

We aren't praying to get something off our chest, we are trying to penetrate and unleash power on a wretched situation. We are not punching a time card; we are pouring onto God the travail and misery of our times.

Someday you will pray unceasingly and an awesome thing will happen that I will describe in the next chapter. For now, your prayers will be in stages of development toward a glorious Upper Room experience.

Wait for a release from the Holy Spirit before you end a time of prayer. Even when we are totally unaware of any result, something is going on in the heavenlies. Something is being created that we can't feel or understand. The angel told Daniel that his voice was heard and a response was on its way from the first moment he set his heart to seek God. "As soon as you began to pray, an answer was given, which I have come to tell you, for you are highly esteemed. Therefore, consider the message and understand the vision." (Daniel 9:23)

We must stay in prayer until God is satisfied that this particular season of prayer has fulfilled its purpose.

Never lose sight of the fact that what you are doing is of life and death importance. There is a real Satan and the casualties in our nation from our lack of prayer are overwhelming.

Nothing you are doing is more important than expending your soul on this kind of praying.

I have been careful to describe the exhaustive experience prayer is so that you won't lose heart when you battle it yourself. However, eventually you will find that time will fly and that persistence will give you breakthroughs. Soon the atmosphere of the place you pray will become glorious. A wonderful sweetness will pervade your soul. After a while your time in prayer will seem so precious that you will long for it and anticipate it with wonder and awe. At first you may have to force yourself to prayer, but soon you will be having to tear yourself away even after God has released you. You simply won't want to leave His presence.

The third aspect of this kind of prayer is that it is also a military act. It is an act against the supreme villain in your neighborhood.

Ephesians 6:12 says that we wrestle against principalities and powers. We are in a state of war against spiritual forces of evil in the heavenly realms. They have rank and it is clearly revealed in scripture that they control specific geographical areas.

There are many definitions for revival. Yet there is one that is central: revival is the defeating of the local demonic authority by prayer. Jesus referred to it as binding the strong man. "Or again, how can anyone enter a strong man's house and carry off his possessions unless he first ties up the strong man?" (Matthew 12:29)

Picture Daniel after weeks of fasting, weak, weary and at the point of collapse. Something beyond hunger is sapping his strength. He is contending in another dimension. Even though he is in Babylon physically, his spirit is travailing in combat on a distant, invisible battlefield. The groanings are coming faster and harder. His prayers intensify to an unbearable level and suddenly there is a burst.

Daniel looks up to see a glorious angelic being that no one else around him can see.

This angel who looks like a man comforts Daniel and explains the delay. The Prince of Persia opposed him twenty-one days. He was detained until Michael the archangel came with reinforcement. "But the prince of the Persian kingdom resisted me twenty-one days. Then Michael, one of the chief princes, came to help me, because I was detained there with the king of Persia." (Daniel 10:13)

Daniel understood the travail. He saw a connection between his prayer and the shattering of the Prince of Persia.

Once Charles Finney traveled through a small village. Its sin and darkness gripped him. Off he went to a private part of the woods to war in prayer against whoever Satan had delegated to this village. Nearly a day went by.

Based on what I have read of Finney, I can imagine that the prayer session was violent. After he praised God and trounced demons, he arose and walked over to a textile factory on the edge of the village. All he did was look at the factory workers and they began to sob for forgiveness from God. Soon an entire village was swept up and into the Kingdom of Jesus Christ.

Joshua and Caleb understood how, in spiritual warfare, that the strong man is bound.

"If the Lord is pleased with us, He will lead us into that land, a land flowing with milk and honey, and will give it to us. Only do not rebel against the Lord. And do not be afraid of the people of this land, because we will swallow them up. Their protection is gone but the Lord is with us." (Numbers 14:8,9)

God goes before us into battle, removing the enemy's protection. He has chosen to honor and limit His intervention to what we pray for.

God looks on, heartbroken and astonished, that only a meager handful of His servants have discovered this mighty tool.

I am certain that our bitterest regret will come when we are in heaven and we see for the first time the real power and privilege of prayer. Our spirits will cry out, saying, "If I had only known, how I would have prayed!"

STAGE FOUR:
Critical mass

If my people, who are called by my name, will humble themselves and pray and **seek my face** *and turn from their wicked ways, then will I hear from heaven and will forgive their sin and will heal their land.*

II Chronicles 7:14

It is my exciting privilege now to open up to you the revelation that caused me to write this book.

The unfolding of this dynamic truth begins in a room. I'm sure that all of us would love to have been in that room. It is the Upper Room in Jerusalem and it is just weeks after the resurrection of Jesus.

One hundred twenty believers are praying and waiting. All they know is that two things are going to happen: (1) the Holy Spirit is going to come upon them; (2) they are going to receive power.

What thoughts must have drifted through their minds as they prayed. What is the Holy Spirit like? What will this power Jesus mentioned feel like? How long will we have to pray?

The commission Jesus gave them before He ascended only added to the uncertainty and anxiety.

They were supposed to go into all the world and preach the gospel. They were barely a local movement; how could they ever become a worldwide movement?

They knew that their mission was born of God, but how tiny and vulnerable they must have seemed to themselves. The little band of Christians had no way to imagine the impact they were about to have on mankind.

The Feast of Pentecost was an annual blowout. Jerusalem was like pre-Super Bowl celebration with United Nations overtones.

From every nation on earth, Jews and those gentiles who embraced Judaism came together and brought their friends to celebrate. If *People* magazine had been around, the celebration might have been reported in this way:

"Jerusalem today is celebrating! Everyone who is anyone is here. Can there be any doubt that Jerusalem right now is the place to be? Along any street you can bump into a celebrity.

"The local religious leadership is anxious to put the terrible events of the last few weeks behind them and show Jerusalem's best side to the world.

"To be sure, the execution of the prophet from Nazareth did threaten to dampen the party, especially the rumors of His rising from the dead. However, the Feast of Pentecost is all anyone is thinking of right now and even Jesus' followers, once very visible, are off mourning somewhere."

No one but God knew how thoroughly and shockingly the tables would be turned.

The unpromising prayer meeting continued on raw obedience. It took grit and courage to stay in the Upper

Room. What a contrast on Pentecost morning! Inside, sober and vigilant saints; outside, a party cranking up. Inside there is supplication; outside, the festive sounds. The exterior laughter and fun seemed to mock them and taunt them into thinking life had passed them by.

Then everyone heard it . . . out of nowhere, a hurricane! A mighty roar that effortlessly drowned out the sounds of the party.

The Holy Spirit roared onto the earth and into the church. The spotlight of history was ripped away from the now unimportant feast outside and it turned to the newly-born world-changers and their tongues of fire.

Like a torrent of white hot lava from a fresh eruption, the believers poured out of the Upper Room and stunned the tens of thousands milling around outside their door.

Riveted ears and eyes beheld that fragile stage prop we call "physical reality" topple as the more real spiritual world took over. Each person heard his own language being spoken by those who couldn't possibly speak it.

For the only time in history, an evangelistic message had bypassed the agency of the preacher's mind; it was worded completely by the Holy Spirit.

Small wonder that 15,000 new believers were added to their number within minutes of the miracle. They had reached critical mass.

The heartbeat and mission of this book is to see the American church reach critical mass again.

Yes, the coming of the Holy Spirit on earth at Pentecost is a one-time event, but subsequent empowerings to the point of shattering Satan and taking over cities are not only possible, they are indispensable.

The issue isn't God's power; it is us. Can we be honest enough to admit we have failed? Can we renounce our pride and face the fact that we have built, in many cases, a Christian corporate conglomerate that has no Upper Room?

Satan has effectively taken us off the battlefield by deceiving us into commemorating the power of Pentecost instead of utilizing it.

There is a path back to power but it is hard to see. It cuts off from the well-worn broad way of mediocre Christian living. It is hard to spot because few have travelled that way lately and weeds have grown over it from years of neglect.

The truth of critical mass has been told to each generation with perhaps different words but always with the same promise. If God's conditions are met, the river of God will flood the land with blessing.

Martin Luther, John Wesley, and Charles Finney all had something in common: they were all proponents of critical mass in their day.

They were feared by established order because they brought change, exposed current hypocrisy, and led the church back to power.

Another similarity was their use of fresh terminology. They polished tarnished silver and gold truths, restoring them to their original brilliance. They reminded the church of her legacy of triumph and demanded that she live up to it.

If we would only quit fearing voices like that today!

These great awakeners who preached and prophesied until revival shook the land knew the secret of power and they knew how to inspire it in others.

To dramatize the demands of God and the glories of present truth, they used analogies from their times.

Imagine a giant like John Wesley alive today in the era of nuclear power. He could not avoid seeing the staggering parallel of nuclear fission and God's process of transforming mere believers into irresistible conduits of "dunamis."

First, there is the very principle of fission itself. To have a chain reaction you must first find the element that is capable of sustaining a chain reaction. This is called fissile material. The only known elements of this kind are uranium and plutonium.

These elements are rare but you don't need much. Likewise, the angel said to Abraham that the presence of only ten righteous people could save Sodom and Gomorrah. "Then he (Abraham) said, 'May the Lord not be angry, but let me speak just once more. What if only ten can be found there?' He answered, 'For the sake of ten, I will not destroy it.' " (Genesis 18:32)

In our country right now, scattered across the land, probably unknown even to themselves, is that core of people that God esteems as being capable of sustaining a spiritual chain reaction.

As long as they stay apart, Satan rejoices. But a signal has gone out that the time for Christians to live in isolation is over, that it is high time to put aside petty doctrinal issues, and restore fierceness to our times of prayer. God's people must quit pointing their rifles at each other and, instead, train them on the devil and then fire in unison.

In nature, fission will not happen unless a minimum

amount and a specific purity of fissile material is present.

Critical mass is that minimum amount . . . but it also is a purity in that amount.

The current Christian generation must allow itself to undergo a dealing of God that resembles an atom being brought to fission. To fully grasp this spiritual understanding, you must see how fission happens. The description I'm about to give is a gross simplification of a highly technical act, but it will be adequate for the purposes of this book.

The power is in the nucleus of the atom. That is why we speak of nuclear power. That power is trapped within the atom until the proper principle is used to release it.

The nucleus of the atom is surrounded by a negative electron cloud and something must penetrate that cloud and agitate the nucleus. What does this is a neutron beam. That beam bombards the atom until the nucleus starts to respond. The physical characteristics of the nucleus completely change. It is now at critical mass.

The key is the penetration of the negative electron cloud by the neutron beam. This uses an incredible amount of energy because the cloud around the nucleus is a powerful shield. Bear this in mind because that cloud is the greatest obstacle to fission, just as its spiritual counterpart is the greatest barrier to revival.

What we seek is nuclear power, in the sense that there is something in us that must be released. Paul said, "Christ in you, the hope of glory." (Colossians 1:27)

Our central verse is II Chronicles 7:14, which we have followed step by step. The previous chapter was about prayer. Critical mass is about seeking the face of God, something beyond prayer.

The verse says, ". . . will humble themselves and pray . . . seek my face." From God's perspective, seeking His face is the same as seeking His glory. The connection between the two is clear in the following example: Moses asked God to "show me your glory." God's response was, "No one can see my face and live." (Exodus 33: 18,20)

In Stage Three, we are praying. In Stage Four, we are seeking the neutron beam of God's glory. In Stage Three, we are sending petitions up to heaven. In Stage Four, heaven starts to bombard us. The nature of the revival core changes; it is at critical mass.

The complete picture of spiritual fission is seen in the story of Gideon. God told Gideon his army was too large. Imagine that! It goes against all principles of war. In only two realms do you decrease the size in order to increase the power . . . nuclear power and spiritual awakening. (See Judges 7)

God was telling Gideon that not all of his men were fissile material and to get rid of all who could not sustain a chain reaction.

The victory of Gideon over the Midianites was even a clearer parallel to critical mass. As they surrounded the camp at night, Gideon ordered each man to place a torch in a clay pot. At Gideon's command, they were to simultaneously shatter the pot and reveal the burning torch within. The impact was astonishing! The Midianites lost heart and ran for their lives, sure that they were being attacked by an army of tens of thousands.

Wasn't the Upper Room a case of critical mass? Although Jesus had thousands of admirers in Jerusalem, the real nuclear material was only 120.

There was even a similarity in the tongues of fire about them. The Bible says, "cloven tongues of fire." Cloven means "split."

Even Jesus refers to the fission-like impact of His coming to earth. "I have come to bring fire on the earth, and how I wish it were already kindled! But I have a baptism to undergo, and how distressed I am until it is completed! Do you think I came to bring peace on earth? No, I tell you, but division (fission)." (Luke 12:51)

The negative electron cloud, the clay pots of Gideon, and our old nature are precisely the same thing . . . a barrier. A barrier that keeps something out and holds something in.

Only the glory of God will bring your revival core to critical mass. Settle it in your heart that as God warned Moses that if he saw God's face it would mean death, so will our exposure to the glory mean the death of pride, lust, and anger. It will shatter the barrier. It will bring revival!

Today's church is so confident in its techniques. We speak of the cutting edge when we refer to some fresh approach or nifty tool for growth. Well, we've had money; we've had new buildings; we've had converted movie stars; we've had just about everything but a genuine impact on a freshly paganized America. We are losing the war where it matters . . . in the secular arena.

We are charming to modern Americans and they know we are conservative. We have impressed them with our organizational abilities and they basically understand our traditions.

Jesus, the doctrine, is common knowledge. America

has been introduced to Jesus on the installment plan, a plan that allows for immunity, not infectious faith.

A breed of believer must arise that will set fire to the dry grass of American religion. Instead of being available "nice guys" the army of God must become the conscience of the nation, a dread of demons, and at last a supernatural river of life for the full spectrum of human pain. Only the glory will do that.

Let's dispense with theories of how to make the church relevant. God doesn't want her merely relevant; He wants her glorious!

Only the coming of the glory will solve our weaknesses. Only the glory of God will crash this end-time party and release millions from Satan.

As long as we entertain the idea that there is a substitute for the glory, we have already surrendered by default. We need that glory that filled the temple and prevented the priests from ministering. We need the glory that made Isaiah cry out, "Here I am, send me."

In cities everywhere, upper rooms must be formed. Groups must gather whose entire purpose is heavenward.

The servant of Elijah returned to find the prophet still in spiritual travail unto birth. He gave Elijah good news. "I see a cloud the size of a man's fist." I see a cloud also, a churning mushroom cloud over America, a cloud of the glory of God! It will come after our prayers have penetrated God and His glory has penetrated us.

Revival, like fission, is a sudden burst of power that is irresistible. That power overwhelms the gates of hell. Satanic hordes flee in total terror before the crashing wave of God. Nothing travels as fast as light and nothing penetrates humanity like righteousness.

To be brought to critical mass is worth everything. Whatever the cost, revival is worth it.

The glory will come; sin will be cleansed. Soon it will start intensifying, barriers will be broken, until suddenly . . . bang! . . . tongues of fire. The sword of God is unsheathed, and the army of God is poured out on a waiting world.

STAGE FIVE:
Dark night of the soul

*If my people, who are called by my name, will humble themselves and pray and seek my face **and turn from their wicked ways,** then will I hear from heaven and will forgive their sin and will heal their land.*

II Chronicles 7:14

Another key similarity between revival and nuclear fission is a strange phenomenon that occurs right before the atom splits. The nucleus actually depresses. Scientists observe that the neutron bombardment, which seemed to be changing the nucleus, now shows no sign of reaching critical mass. Nothing seems to be happening.

That is also what happens right before a manifestation of God's glory. The revival core will be praying and sensing a rising tide of power and expectancy. All of a sudden, you hit a brick wall. The power is gone. God's presence seems to have lifted. Your prayers feel trapped in your mouth. A deep despair settles in. You feel physically drained.

This is the dark night of the soul. This is where every revival pioneer has been before you and now it's your turn. It will take everything in you to keep moving. The sobering fact is that many who have reached the dark night of the soul have retreated. Eternity will reveal a long, sad history of revival near-misses.

Let me state emphatically that 90 percent of revival is getting to the point where an unshakable resolve is born. Everything you have done before you reach this dark night will seem unimportant. It is what you do now that makes or breaks your heart's desire.

At no other point does God express love more than when He allows this time of total emptiness. God risks being misunderstood. He faces the potential of one of His children walking away frustrated and confused, but He believes the good it will produce is well worth the risk.

What do you do when this cloud of darkness settles on you?

Scientists respond to a depressed nucleus by intensifying the neutron beam, and resolve to do so until fission occurs. They commit to keep moving, not relying on any physical signs. That is precisely what we must do to see the end of this night.

Why does God allow this dark night? I strongly believe that our Father realized that those through whom He works to bring revival receive great praise from the church and awesome attacks of Satan. A person lacking humility won't survive the praise of men. A person without perseverance won't overcome Satan. The revival core must realize this and stand the test.

Just as a scientist turns up the force of the neutron beam even though he sees no result, so true revivalists will turn up their prayer during the dark night of the soul. If the children of God demonstrate that they won't go by what they see or feel, God will know that He has vessels that can be trusted with revival. In the heat of battle, they will not rely on circumstances or feelings to keep them on a straight course.

If the prayer of the revival core continues during this dark night, their true motive surfaces. The only thing that will hold us when the nucleus depresses is a pure heart of love for the lost and a true desire to see God glorified. God wisely observes that anyone who survives this night is rightfully suited to invade enemy territory.

Again we see this fifth stage in our key verse, II Chronicles 7:14, "... will humble themselves and pray, seek my face, and turn from their wicked ways ..."

It would seem that by this stage, God would know we have abandoned our sin. The issue, however, is something deeper; it deals with our ways.

Our repentance has dealt with what we have done; now the purification focuses on what we *are*.

The psalmist distinguished two aspects of God: His acts and His ways. "He made known his *ways* to Moses, his deeds to the people of Israel." (Psalm 103:7)

The children of Israel only knew God from miracle to miracle, but Moses knew the deep intentions and the long-range plan of God. Moses understood the essence, heartbeat, and direction of God.

To turn from our wicked ways doesn't just mean to repent of our sins. Hitherto, we have repented of our acts; now we need deliverance from our ways.

Gethsemane was the dark night of the soul for Jesus Christ; it was the test of His ways. You wonder if Jesus had to repent. The answer is no, but He had to be examined in His Father's court of justice.

The dark night of the soul is a very baffling test, for it comes at the least expected time and with special conditions. The inner nature must be surprised, caught off guard, in order to be exposed and conquered.

In the many records of revival, there is an almost uniform description of this crucible . . . on the mountaintop one moment, feeling run over by a train the next.

Joseph, barely recovered from a glorious dream, is thrown into a pit by his brothers. David, still hearing the chant of the throng saying, "Saul has slain his thousands and David his ten thousands," wakes up in a cave being hunted like an animal.

Even Jesus, with the hosannas still ringing in His ears from His triumphal entry into Jerusalem, now prays alone, cold, tormented, sweating blood, and surrounded by sleeping disciples.

The battlements of heaven are waiting for that unmistakable ring of genuine obedience where the dragon of human nature has been met and beheaded. "Not my will but thy will be done!"

Before the crown comes the cup. It must be swallowed to the bitter dregs.

So then, what is the Lord really looking for? A servant who knows that the cup cannot pass. Take heart if you wish that it would pass. Even Jesus asked if it was necessary to drink. But He did not ask to escape because of fear of pain or selfishness. He asked because, for the first time in eternity, He would be separated from His Father. He knew that the plan to save man would have to break His Father's heart. Only Abraham and Isaac on Mount Moriah could begin to understand the grief.

Herein lies the truth that releases the glory. In repenting of sin, we rid ourselves of evil but in the dark night of the soul, we surrender the things we dearly love, things we can't readily identify as being in conflict with God.

Here the issue is not right and wrong, but high and low purposes of living.

Spiritual awakening is not simply getting rid of sin, it is giving God what He wants.

Again and again I have tried to stress that we must conclude with iron resolve that there is no substitute for revival. It is that higher ground we must reach because the flood is rising. No point of return can exist, no alternative can be considered.

For fire to fall and consume the sacrifice, it must be innocent and without blemish but, most of all, it must be on the altar to stay.

Under every other circumstance our nature can hide, but in this dark night it screams for its way, and its many tentacles are exposed.

Mary took the alabaster box filled with rich ointment, broke it, and poured the wondrously fragrant contents on Jesus.

The protest was immediate. "Why this waste?" screamed the disciples, led by Judas Iscariot. Their outrage was almost convincing. The ointment was worth a year's salary (maybe $12,000 today). It could have fed the poor, they argued (actually, Judas wanted to steal it).

This is the entire issue of revival. They wanted to do

something for God. Mary knew it was time to do something to God.

The time has come to pour out our best on God. Jesus said, "The poor you have with you always." Good deeds are always available.

America is spiritually dying because God has sales reps and not channels of His glory. We feverishly do the right things, almost as a bribe to postpone the needed pouring out of ourselves on God as a living sacrifice.

Again, we must no longer see the bad things as barriers to revival, but the seemingly good.

We can't dole out precious ointment to the poor in doses that don't cure them or honor God. We must be poured out on God!

Spiritual awakening means that the faithful become fiery, the decent become dynamic, and the acceptable become excellent. But, most of all, we become disgusted with our evil, and totally dissatisfied with our good.

We realize that now is the time to pull out all the stops. No program is sacred, no worthy project is worth enough. None of the ointment can be spared. It is revival or death!

As I said before, the nucleus of the atom depresses right before fission and in that lies another key parallel to revival . . . the nucleus explodes from that depressed condition. It does not split when it looks inflated and energetic but rather when it is shrunken and lifeless.

Revival comes out of nowhere by sovereign timing. The prayer core is ready to fall from exhaustion but hangs on by its confidence in the faithfulness of God.

Jehovah detects that special quality that can be rewarded with revival.

An eviction notice falls with a loud crash on the porch of the local satanic supervisor. Angels receive their invasion orders. The prayer core looks up and sees the glory coming. The roar of God is about to be heard in the land once more!

STAGE SIX:
The steel punch of God

If my people, who are called by my name, will humble themselves and pray and seek my face and turn from their wicked ways, **then will I hear from heaven and will forgive their sin** *and will heal their land.*

II Chronicles 7:14

David Brainerd found a place to pray that few of us would choose . . . under a bush in two feet of snow during subzero temperatures.

He was not a masochist. He was a man obsessed with the plight of the Appalachian Indians. They were wretchedly poor, spiritually destitute tribes, stripped of their homeland. They barely survived these winters in their makeshift dwellings. God made them the focus of David Brainerd's compassion, and there under that bush he poured himself out on their behalf. Cold, exhausted, and ill, Brainerd began to cough up blood.

Then he reached that crucial point where self is overcome and critical mass is achieved. Brainerd was startled by new strength. Suddenly he felt a vast victory had been won. Instinctively, he rose and ran to the village, where he beheld one of the most marvelous sights in recorded history.

The Indians were standing outside their dwellings, sobbing, unaware of the cause for their tears. As Brainerd approached them, an astonishing thing happened. A hot wind knocked several to the ground; anyone who came near the preacher instantly fell to the ground.

Imagine the joy! Imagine the glory! The Indians embraced this man as an angel from God and they made Jesus their Master.

This is Sixth Stage of revival: the steel punch of God. It has happened in each revival and its manifestation literally creates a circle of radioactivity that levels with conviction anyone who enters it.

In the great awakening in New England, there was an actual point off the shore of America extending a few miles out to sea that was a force field. Once entered, it sent crews and passengers on ships into conviction and repentance. It was common to see those newly converted disembark weeping for joy at their salvation!

At Azusa Street, Brother Seymour and his faithful prayer warriors were told by Satan that they were ignorant, poor nobodies, praying in the wrong part of Los Angeles. They only thought of God and His promise. They reached critical mass and 1,000 nights of glory began. The Pentecostal revival was born and now covers the world. It is staggering to realize that Pentecostal fire spread, until today it makes up nearly half of all Christians worldwide and the world's largest churches.

Now it's your turn. Weeping may endure for a night but joy comes in the morning!

Now it seems like ages since you began your vigil and you are not the same person you were even a prayer ago. You and those who pray with you are at a magnificent point. Something is going to happen!

You have weathered the worst and can't imagine abandoning your post now. If nothing else, you are thrilled to finally know Jesus is your Lord and that your body no longer dictates the depth of your walk with God.

You have reached that historic point of no return. You and your prayer group cannot be denied!

God has found an altar that can have the fire. Your prayers are building a monument before God just as the angel said to Cornelius. "Cornelius stared at him in fear. 'What is it, Lord?' he asked. The angel answered, 'Your prayers and gifts to the poor have come up as a remembrance before God.' " (Acts 10:4)

Something is happening in the regions of hell and something is churning in the heavenlies.

All the prayers are mounting a case before God. It is time for favor to be shown in your city. Mercy is about to take on muscle. A strategy is being drawn. The angelic host has been summoned before God to receive orders. Soon they will charge and bind the strong man. The demonic hierarchy is about to be routed.

Spirits of pornography, prostitution and violence will feel the cutting edge of the sword of the Lord. What is about to happen is the steel punch of God.

In all my years of preaching, nothing has frustrated me more than to see an entire generation that does not know the fullness of the glory of God. With all of our fine concerts, youth events, well-programmed meetings, and services, we simply haven't seen the steel punch.

What this lack of glory has reaped is heartbreaking.

Most don't believe a God-given takeover is possible. It is not preached or advocated by those who should be the principal advocates of revival.

To the list of those who need to see the glory of God, I add myself. Oh, yes, I've seen outbreaks here and there, but not what my heart truly yearns to see. But the point is, I believe it! I am expectant of God's power, not suspicious of it.

Do not misunderstand me. While I say this generation has not seen the full glory of God, I am not saying we haven't seen significant breakthroughs. Quite the contrary; we are so close now that if a tidal wave of righteousness does not come crashing in on America, I'll be shocked. Winkie Pratney in his book *Revival* compares the sudden shockwave of revival with a battle between Israel and Syria where Israel used a legendary tactic called the "steel punch." The Russians served as advisors to the Syrians. The idea was put forth to place over a million land mines in concentric circles, creating an impenetrable wall. However, Israel is no normal army. They devised a plan that is now legendary in military tactics.

They gathered every piece of heavy equipment they could find, tractors, tanks, and large trucks. Then they advanced on the Golan Heights in a single column. As the front of the column would hit mines and explode, the rest of the column would merely plow it out of the way and keep advancing. The Syrians were astounded as the Israelis pierced through and defeated them.

The steel punch of God is a focused church, a church that pierces Satan's hordes as a single fist, not limp fingers that wiggle in all directions.

Only the glory of God can make us that.

Until the dream becomes a plan and you begin to live out the promise that He will hear from heaven, all I have said is just words on paper.

No one realizes more than I how unreal such an act of God in our times seems. But do not succumb; do not doubt.

Habakkuk personifies the position and prayer of the church in anticipation of a miracle. "Lord, I have heard of your fame; I stand in awe of your deeds, O Lord. Renew them in our day, in our time make them known; in wrath remember mercy." (Habakkuk 3:2)

But what really happens in the spiritual dimension when the steel punch of God occurs? It is a very precise victory that we desperately need to understand.

Jesus taught us to pray, ". . . Thy will be done on earth as it is in heaven." (Luke 11:2) This leads us to conclude that by prayer, the order, joy, and authority of God can be transferred to specific areas of earth! A London reporter explained the Welsh revival in that very way. He said that an unearthly sensation could be felt the moment you came into Wales! The feeling was both one of dread of God and yet joy at sensing God's presence.

Somehow the church has lost sight of the general hold that demonic power has over a neighborhood. That hold blinds and confuses its victims. "The god of this age has blinded the minds of unbelievers, so that they cannot see the light of the gospel of the glory of Jesus Christ, who is the image of God." (II Corinthians 4:4)

Presently a deliberate, sophisticated conspiracy exists. It cruelly submerges people's minds in confusion and misunderstanding. Its goal is to prevent the good news of who Jesus really is from being seen. Invisible liars infest our land, biasing everyone against Christ.

Imagine what would happen if the lie was suddenly exposed and the anti-Jesus bias was revoked. Consider this analogy. After a long and bitter court fight, the court rules in your favor. The press is convicted of libel, slander, and malicious intent. The lies that were printed and spoken must be retracted and the very avenues of the press itself must be put at your disposal until the court deems the wrong to be righted. That's it! The steel punch of God is a divine verdict that orders the lie to stop, the eyes of the blinded are opened, the true glory of Jesus is plainly seen by an entire community.

Not everyone is going to be saved but this punch releases the victims of the lie and many of them will charge immediately into the kingdom of Christ. Those who do not, at least have seen the pure gospel and stand before God without excuse.

Remember, Satan is mortally wounded since Calvary, so he relies on his expert knowledge of human nature to deceive. He is bereft of power and therefore en-snares by the use of illusion. That illusion disintegrates once the punch of God's power strikes.

I want to remind you of the specific words of the angel of Daniel when he said, "The prince of Persia opposed me twenty-one days." (Daniel 10:13) In Stage Three I told you about the connection between our prayer and the piercing of regional strongholds of de-mons. Now let's look closer at the role of angels in this act of defeating Satan.

Angels are given orders to guard the heirs of eternal

life. They also long to attack Satan's forces, which they do very effectively. In fact, in Revelation an angel that is not of very high rank is ordered to go and bind Satan for a thousand years. But angels are dependent on prayer! Standing watch right now, even as you read this book, is an angelic host that is assigned to your area!

The second and third chapters of Revelation are actually letters written to the archangel assigned to a specific church. That angel knows the demonic strong man in our area, the same way that American soldiers stationed on the border of North and South Korea know their communist counterpart.

Our intercession arms that angel. Think of it! That angel hates that local demon and doubtless that angel has rehearsed over and over how he would punch that demon's lights out if only our prayers would fuel him.

Because the angels of God are eternal beings, they have a special desire to attack Satan and his minions. The angels of God saw the brutal slaying of Jesus. They watched helplessly as Jesus was tortured and murdered and this is their chance to exact vengeance on Satan! Satan is their greatest point of hatred and we must be their greatest point of frustration! The reason revival strikes with such force is because, when these beautiful, obedient warriors get the chance, they attack with total abandon.

Why have these principles been so ignored by the modern church? Because American Christians have lost their heart for war! Arthur Mathews declared that "an escapist generation is baffled by the thought of attacking Satan."

The steel punch is a military act. Because we do not

view ourselves as soldiers or the Christian life as a war, we don't know our rights, we don't study our weapons, and we don't realize the humiliating blow we can deal the devil!

The death of Jesus does not affect us the way it does angels. We don't have an indelible mark on our memory of the vicious killing of the most precious One. Isaiah wailed, "Who will declare his generation? for he was cut off from the land of the living." (Isaiah 53:8 KJV)

Paul learned to carry the vengeance of the angels when he said he was "always bearing about in my body the dying of the Lord Jesus." (II Corinthians 4:10 KJV)

Let us now turn from angels to the supreme cause of the steel punch: the steel puncher, the Holy Spirit.

This consistently overlooked member of the Trinity is God and He carries the power, the plan, and the weapons of spiritual awakening.

II Corinthians 10:4 says, "The weapons of our warfare are not carnal but are mighty through God to the tearing down of strongholds." (KJV)

As commander-in-chief of Jesus Christ's armed forces, the Holy Spirit administrates a vast arsenal of weapons and gifts all purchased by the death of Jesus Christ.

All of these gifts and weapons have a central attitude and characteristic. They derive this attitude from the Person that gives them. Since the Holy Spirit gives them, these gifts reflect His resolve for victory and His determination to tear down strongholds of Satan. The U.S. Air Force has rockets with aiming devices. Some of them are heat-seeking rockets, others are aimed by lasers. The gifts of the Spirit also have aiming devices and herein lies a secret of power and the explanation of our powerlessness.

The Holy Spirit and His gifts are mighty. In all honesty, we cannot declare with Paul that "the weapons of our warfare are not carnal," because they are. We use human weapons on supernatural problems. Our little weekend talks and charming parade of Sunday antics are a flagrant denial of both the ongoing war and the Holy Spirit's intention to win it.

The key is the attitude of the Spirit and His gifts. They are mighty to the tearing down of strongholds. They are not mighty if they are not aimed at demon nests.

The gifts of the Spirit cease to operate when they are squandered on the already fattened saints.

A local church is only as powerful as its commitment to attack local satanic activity. When foolish reasons for existing are abandoned, and backslidden board members are no longer feared, once pastors turn from timid talks to ordering the troops to attention, when there is thundered from the pulpit the blazing truth of our inheritance, and the utter outrage of Lucifer's pillaging of our city, then and only then can we align ourselves with the intention of the commander-in-chief to tear down strongholds. Finally, we will understand the might of the weapons of God.

Our lack of understanding of the steel punch is the product of incomplete teaching on the cross of Jesus Christ.

You can trace the lack of dynamic impact of the church on society to a specific emphasis on only the atoning death of Jesus. This, of course, is important because the death of Jesus purchased our salvation.

But the cross was not just that. The cross had an active and passive aspect to it. Isaiah said, "He opened not his mouth." Jesus laid down his life. This is the passive lamb slain for mankind whose blood silenced the punishment we deserved.

But the cross was even more! A marvelous military tactic was employed on Satan that must be understood. Let me explain. Adam's fall not only gave us a sin nature, it created a marriage with mankind and Satan. That marriage cannot be broken except by death. (Romans 7:4) Jesus had to perform two vital acts in one act. Our fallen nature can never please God; therefore, we must be eternally separated from God and by virtue of our spiritual marriage to Satan, we were not even free to choose God.

Simultaneously, on the cross Jesus gave us His nature which does please God and then took our cursed bondage to Satan by becoming sin. "For he hath made him to be sin for us, who knew no sin; that we might be made the righteousness of God in him." (II Corinthians 5:21 KJV)

To understand the act of Jesus on the cross, you must also see the authority of Adam that was stolen. Adam could have thrown the serpent out of the Garden. The earth was Adam's. He was given power to subdue it and replenish it. When Adam gave it away, Satan became master of earth. The Bible says, "The whole world lies in the evil one." (I John 5:19) Adam had merely to command Satan and the serpent would cower before Him because Adam was a son of God!

Now put the picture together. Jesus was the second Adam, dying on the cross, taking upon Himself the punishment of the first Adam and his descendants.

Imagine Satan controlling Judas so that the Son of Man is betrayed. Satan thinks to himself, "I can't believe I got away with this." He is emboldened to turn all of Jerusalem against Jesus and murder Him. Satan falsely concludes that God is weak and that killing Jesus is the next step in his fiendish plan to dethrone God.

He has no idea that killing Jesus is the last thing he should do. Jesus the man dies and is free from the curse because He is dead. Jesus the God in man comes back from the dead and on His way back, Jesus does what Adam should have done. Jesus strips Satan of power and sentences him to the lake of fire. The Bible says in Colossians 2:14, 15, "Having cancelled the written code, with its regulations, that was against us and that stood opposed to us; he took it away, nailing it to the cross. And having disarmed the powers and authorities, he made a public spectacle of them, triumphing over them by the cross!"

It is clear that the cross was to Satan a total shock and defeat. He simply did not know what a mistake it was to crucify Jesus.

For the church to understand the steel punch of God, it must understand the cross. The cross was the ultimate steel punch of God! Once this is understood, we can then see how, in revival, that the sudden penetration of enemy fortresses is an extension of the original punch on the cross. The steel punch of God is a continuance of the disarming of, and exposing to public humiliation, the demon authorities.

The generations of Christians that have only seen the passive act of the cross have been passive themselves about revival, but every generation that has seen the military act of the cross on Satan has gone on to obtain revival!

"For this cause was the son of man manifested; that He might destroy the works of the devil!" (I John 3:8)

"Since the children have flesh and blood, he too shared in their humanity so that by his death he might destroy him who holds the power of death—that is, the devil!" (Hebrews 2:14)

It is no wonder that in 25 revivals I examined, all experienced Stage Six of revival: a sudden, piercing of satanic power that created an area of radiation that brought dread and joy upon everyone who entered it.

That is why we do not lose heart! Our prayers and worship do affect God; they do arm angels and they do release the Holy Spirit.

Once more Satan will be forced to suffer the consequences of the cross: a fresh steel punch of God!

STAGE SEVEN:
Making revival permanent

If my people, who are called by my name, will humble themselves and pray and seek my face and turn from their wicked ways, then will I hear from heaven and will forgive their sin **and will heal their land.**

II Chronicles 7:14

One day Jesus was confronted by a horrible sight. A father, bearing a hopelessly demon-possessed boy, pleaded for help from the disciples. Finding none, he finally turned to Jesus.

The moment the demon sensed the presence of Jesus, he threw the boy to the ground. The boy's face contorted and he writhed in convulsive agony. The demonic spirit proceeded to tear him from the inside out. Then Jesus rebuked the spirit and the boy lapsed into perfect peace.

Everyone began celebrating, but not Jesus . . . not yet! Jesus then *healed* the boy. The moment of relief everyone felt made them overlook an extremely important fact: the boy, though delivered, was still weak and torn. But Jesus lovingly made him normal and healthy. (See Mark 9:17–27)

I've used this account of Jesus to illustrate the incredible significance of the move of revival from Stage Six to Stage Seven. We now venture into a truth that is central to Satan's defeat. Satan does not fear revival nearly as much as he fears our discovery of the fact that revival can be permanent.

In Stage Six, God hears and forgives; in Stage Seven, He heals the land. I believe there is a distinction between God's promise to forgive our sin and His promise to heal our land. The steel punch of God is felt because God has heard and forgiven. The foreign agent in our system is yanked out, but now a void exists. Nowhere in the progressive stages of revival is the temptation to let up greater than it is between Stages Six and Seven. Our theme verse could even read nicely without the ending: ". . . and will heal their land." It could read: ". . . then will I hear from heaven and will forgive their sin . . ." period.

Ironically, at this point the euphoria associated with revival becomes its greatest enemy. Thousands are getting saved; everyone feels God, so why not simply revel in it? People abuse the excitement. They miss work, let school fall behind, and even neglect their marriages . . . all in the name of revival. If Satan can't beat revival, he'll join it by provoking us to a counterfeit emotionalism.

Revival is not an altered state. The steel punch of God is a temporary explosion meant to evolve into permanent patterns of living in revival. This abuse is meant by the enemy to cause us to wear out physically and to lead us into extremes that will discredit the awakening in the eyes of the public.

We must stay keenly aware of the possibility that we

subconsciously fear the revival may go away and, as a result of this fear, we allow ourselves to frantically pursue something counterfeit. Our faith in God's character must be intact. Then we can say, "Praise God, this isn't going to go away, so I'll take the time to keep my body healthy, my grades up. I'll keep a healthy witness at work, and I'll take this glory into my marriage." Revival is not fragile! It doesn't simply evaporate.

The Upper Room was a milestone for the Church of Jesus Christ. As I said earlier in this book, it was there that the believers reached critical mass. However, after the tongues of fire, something happened of equal or even greater importance . . . the long-awaited demonstration of the church in action. The power of the steel punch of God to get a city's attention is awesome, but the real impact, the real catalyst to changing a city, is the Body of Christ functioning on a daily basis. After we obtain revival, we must contain revival. We must make the newfound glory a way of life.

The purpose of this chapter is to teach how to make revival permanent. First, we have to brush away the cobwebs on our theology. We must discern our biblical inheritance, especially when it goes against the grain of our experience and the way religious leadership has "minded the store" in the age of technology.

Our self-image has been so battered by our sophisticated modern age that we regard token responses to Christ as real progress. We dilute the revolutionary transformation demanded by God to a palatable request that people improve themselves by coming forward. Jesus is not a momentary relief from the stress of modern life. He is the leader of a cosmic prison break. He is not here to redecorate people's jail cells, but rather to be the king of a new kingdom that exists in this world but is not of this world. The entire motive that energizes a believer in Christ is absolutely foreign to this world.

We, the church, have erroneously assumed that the more like modern man we make Christianity look, the more it will be accepted. The fact is, most people know that humanism doesn't work and, frankly, they are sick of it. When the world comes near us, we don't realize how much radicalism they've already tried. They've used drugs, they've dyed their hair purple, they've done most of what there is to do. That is why they are so disappointed in us when they approach the church. Instead of a revolutionary call to a new kingdom, they hear echoes of humanism. They hear apologetics from Christian intellectuals who exclaim we are almost as smart as secular thinkers. They hear Christian bands that make the same repetitious, unoriginal sounds as Top 40 Radio.

Our uniqueness is gone . . . our "otherworldness." When E. T. arrived, he was adored by millions because he was not of this world and he showed how stupid and boring modern life was. That pent-up adoration that E. T. touched properly belonged to Christ, but the church was not "extraterrestrial" enough to capture it.

This is not to say we should be spooky or mystical. It is simply to say we should be ourselves. We are supposed to be a bride for the most glorious Bridegroom in the universe.

The Bible was given to us to fashion a culture within a culture—a life-force to confront a lifestyle. We need supernatural unselfishness, not a "born-again" greed passed off as gospel to a market of greedy Americans. We should have an elation derived from tasting holiness—a living purity, not empty rules that are put on us like chains. We need a divine distraction where sin becomes boring and hated for its effect on God, whom we desperately love. When we soft-pedal God's demand for holiness, we lie about Him and us. We imply He has no right to ask for it when, in fact, without it, we won't even see Him. We lie about ourselves if we act as if being holy is dreary. If we could see clearly what the scriptures teach, we would conclude that holiness and righteousness are the highest pleasures a human spirit can contain.

The world longs for an example! If only they could see someone who has truly had the boulder of guilt taken off by the justifying power of Jesus, someone infused with the Holy Spirit who has awakened to total harmony with the universe that eastern religion can only fantasize about. If only the world could finally see in a human life a raw injection of Jesus . . . His values, joy, wisdom, originality, peace, and strength. They would see a new person, made alive by God, with eyes that reflect a clear pool of purpose, a heart that beats calmly and securely in the midst of crisis, a voice strong but gentle with advice on the eternal and, most of all, a countenance that is never far away from a celebration of what it means to be redeemed.

Let us then cast off the lie that we must add disclaimers to the gospel. Let us spit out the tendency to apologize for the hope that lies within us. Do we fear what the press would say if we were to truly abandon ourselves to Christ? Forget it! Modern man doesn't believe the press. Do we hold back for fear that a call for strong faith might offend the lukewarm, sedate, well-to-do who underwrite the church budget? Never!!! In actual fact, the "fat cats" have never been the financial power of the church but, rather, the people who are strong in faith and consistent in their giving, and are waiting for revival right now! They want to support a revival and are looking for leadership that is brave enough to be different and bold enough to take God at His Word.

Are we afraid of being misunderstood or thought of as crazy? How ridiculous! Never has society been so completely bored with business as usual and so ready for an injection of radical sanity!

Yes, Peter had to explain that "these are not drunk as you suppose" (see Acts 2:15) but that momentary misunderstanding gave way to a clear witness of power. God would do the same for us if we could discard our excuses and brave that momentary time of being thought of as crazy. To be sure, the disciples did not do it on their own initiative or as a show of peculiarity. They merely rode the wave of Holy Spirit power as it crashed in on a society.

The point is that God saw their willingness. He saw that they would gladly risk the embarrassment of being used of God if it would end in love from heaven embracing a wretched world. Can God see that love in us? It cannot come until we repent of what is really wrong with us as American Christians. We have tried to settle into a cultural mutation of the gospel. Subconsciously, we have written off our world. We believe it is getting worse and that we can't do anything about it. In fact, we believe it is supposed to get worse and be allowed to rot. To ease our consciences, we have accepted this as a time to calmly and passively wait for the rapture. We have even condoned a sort of "tailgate party" as a lead-up to Armageddon. We can, we reason, be an island of believers who sample the less wicked pleasures of our current age and yet wear the badge of safe conduct to heaven. We naively presume we have safely combined the best of two worlds, the last tasty morsels of a dying age, and a disarmed discipleship that requires only a weekly recharging. The disastrous fact is that we mingle two worlds that are at enmity with each other . . . like nitro and glycerin, we can only expect a toxic explosion.

Once again I want to rehearse the impact on the unsaved on the Day of Pentecost. We have a record of a uniquely marvelous event. The Spirit has fallen with such force that the 120 literally poured out into the streets under its current.

As I said before, the impact of the gospel was reinforced because it was being preached, not in men's words as they sought to represent God, but by the direct wording of the Spirit by words the disciples couldn't have known, but was a language that was known intimately by the hearers. Luke says in Acts 2:7 that the people were utterly amazed. And why not? These were humble Galileans. How could they grasp the dialect, the accent, and the idioms of so many cultures so perfectly? Notice what the Spirit said when He was allowed to preach unfettered by human opinion. The crowd exclaimed that they heard the wonders of

God being declared in their own language (see Acts 2:8).

I am convinced that this is where modern gospel preaching falls down. We do not preach the wonder, the magnitude, the all-sufficient majesty of God. The reason that our calls for holiness seem so unreasonable to the modern mind is that they are set against the backdrop of a God who appears puny, moody, divided, fickle and mysteriously distant.

On the Day of Pentecost, God looked huge, nearby and, in a good sense, ominous. The hearers wanted both relief from the terror of God being so close, and yet wanted to be even closer and wanted to worship Him with abandonment. They were at once pierced by His holy presence and drawn by His limitless love. The gospel exposed a present threat and presented an opportunity for a form of life never imagined. It touched every level of their consciousness. But they didn't know what to do! It was a key moment!

While God so wondrously worked, He still placed a sacred trust in the apostles. They had to know how to channel the fresh, innocent devotion to God so that the church could be born healthy and then grow. Acts 2:42 begins with, "They devoted themselves ..." Total unbridled, unconfined repentance and love toward God must have been among those thousands of new converts.

Here is the raw material for God's greatest project to be completed ... a functioning life agency called the Body of Christ whose very presence terrifies Satan and sends forth life in all directions in gentle, daily doses. The description of that community in Acts 2 shows the greatest neighborhood the world has ever seen. This is a clear example of Stage Seven of revival: the church in session, the Body at work!

Jesus said, "I am the vine, you are the branches . . ." (John 15:5) How wondrously do those branches extend to a wounded planet. The church's truth travels at the speed of light; its voice can penetrate all barriers and its gospel is as effective as the resurrection! The question is, can we make that all-important leap to this seventh stage where revival, which has just exploded, is contained? Can we move from a radioactive mushroom cloud to coherent radiation, from a fireball to a laser?

To do so, we must learn what the first century church learned. Remember, they were also human beings, as related in the book of Acts, and in many ways they had less advantages than we have. We too can be touched by the same mixture of fear of God and wonder at His love. As I looked closely at those key verses in Acts 2:42–47, I noticed nine characteristics that highlighted the seventh stage of revival. Three of these dealt with an attitude the people possessed: devotion, expectancy and worship. These qualities are the groundwork for continued revival. A church that wants to sustain revival must have all three attributes.

DEVOTION: They must have a devotion that says, "I'm through with the world and dead religion and I'm determined to serve God and grow, on a daily basis."

EXPECTANCY: They must have a sense of divine expectancy, an attitude of sacred excitement in which the gifts of God are expected and respected. We must also keep our first love, one in which the childlike magic of God's presence never wears off. We must never become casual or cynical about the acts of the

Holy Spirit.

WORSHIP: The third aspect of that attitude is worship. When I visit a church, nothing reveals its condition before God faster than how the people worship. Often a pastor will try to justify his people by saying, "My people are just quiet, they prefer a dignified service." Too often, the real reason is a coldness of spirit toward God. There is nothing wrong with quietness when it is ordered of God and certainly, noise can be empty of worship. But the attitude must be right. We must realize that we are gathered to worship God; our motive should be satisfying Him. True worship is to connect with God's heart and move through praise, sensitive to what pleases Him, and to deepen it until He is blessed. How simply David put it, "Bless the Lord, O my soul; all my inmost being, bless His holy name." (Psalm 103:1)

A church tells Jesus a lot by how the people handle that precious time when He is worshipped. If they merely plow through it, the Holy Spirit senses it and becomes uneasy. If we cut off worship before God is blessed, we will frustrate Him and the acts of power He wished to display among us will be limited.

I believe that leadership sets the tone of worship in a body of believers. There is nothing a pastor can do that is more important than to foster and protect a spirit of true worship among His congregation. We must remember the attitude of the early believers, the state of heart and mind that was perfect for housing a continual act of God: devotion, expectancy, worship.

Now, let us examine the next set of instructions the apostles gave the people. There are three things they were to do continually which would result in unlimited growth in spirit, wisdom, prosperity, and added souls. As the following acts were performed with the right attitude, God would bless. They are:

(1) Training in Christian character (sanctification)
(2) Service to the body and mankind
(3) Prayer

TRAINING: Training has already been defined in the introduction of this book. Training is more than just teaching; it is instruction that demands the student's performance as well. People in revival realize that a deep principle of sin inhabits their nature. They realize that a daily work of God's grace is needed to conquer it. Each day presents a new challenge to let Christ be formed in us. Simply stated, we must continually repent. Charles Finney said that revival is a constant state of repentance. However, it is not an insecure, daily admission of guilt with no hope of success! To understand this, you must be fully aware of justification. When Jesus brought us to the Father, our faith in Christ allowed Jesus to clothe us in His own righteousness. Far more than presentable, we were granted absolute entrance into the presence of God. We were made family, and the issue of belonging was settled.

To grow in God, we must see that nothing threatens God's love and acceptance of us in Christ. *Justification took care of what we did, but now that we're home safe and sound, sanctification addresses what we are* . . . an entity of two radical opposites.

In us lives the embryo of Jesus Christ's character as well as a former nature that bitterly hates God. The roots of that old nature go far deeper than anyone but God can imagine. Were we to see this ugly mass in its full bloom, we would sink into absolute guilt and despair. That is why God deals with it Himself. Only in His love and unconditional acceptance can surgery on our sinful nature be performed. We are to submit to God daily. He will bring into focus a part of our old nature every day and as we repent in faith, we can move on, forgiven and improved.

It is very important that we remember that God considers us healthy, whole, and obedient, not because our old nature is completely conquered, but because we have repented of what God has revealed today. Condemnation will set in when an impatient believer starts to tamper with his soul and gets ahead of God. Satan will gladly help you see your faults in order to crush you. When he does, you must order him away by declaring that God is not holding you accountable to that yet, and you will repent of it when He tells you to. Remember, if God reveals a flaw, it is in the light of His loving power to change you.

The threat to revival occurs when Christians don't believe they have a nature to be changed by God. Sanctification is not built in at conversion; it is separate and its pursuit is lifelong. If we are not engaged in it, we are not pursuing God and the revival is over.

Christian training is simply determining on a daily basis to cooperate with God in becoming everything we can be for Him, at His pace, and under the care of His coaches!

SERVICE: The next feature of Stage Seven is service to Christians and mankind. From the moment that God first asked Cain where Abel was, God has made it plain that a large portion of His blessing to us rides on how we treat others. It's a truth that has been ignored because early in this century, Satan won a major battle against us. When the dual blow of evolution and modern theology stripped the church of confidence and direction, those who stayed true tended to run and hide. False Christians who didn't know God took up the banner of social action. They fed, clothed and cared for the underprivileged, but gave them no gospel.

When the true historians saw this "social gospel," they correctly rejected it as false. However, in our zeal to attack the "social gospel," we lost sight of the real gospel. Central to the message of Jesus was to touch the whole man with the whole message. The cure for the "social gospel" is the demonstration of the real church. However, in our recent tradition, it is almost frowned upon to emphasize helping the needy in our own communities. Yet, there is no way to sustain revival without pleasing God in this way. The biblical evidence is overwhelming. There is no way to adequately address all that the Bible says about this, but a close look at some central verses is absolutely required. Proverbs 21:13 states, "If a man shuts his ears to the cry of the poor, he too will cry out and not be answered." The Word clearly and literally connects our openness to human need as a prerequisite to answered prayer.

But Jesus speaks even more emphatically in Matthew 25:44, 45: "They also will answer, 'Lord, when did we see you hungry or thirsty or a stranger or needing clothes or sick or in prison and did not help you?' He will reply, 'I tell you the truth, whatever you did not do for one of the least of these, you did not do for me.'"

It is obvious that God takes our indifference to the

needy very personally. I should also add that we find no record of the apostles deliberately legislating good works in Acts 2, but the people seemed to know that it was right and that a demonstration of generosity was needed to express their pent-up gratitude to God for new life. *Again, the attitude fueled the act.* Paul must have known this when he said in Romans 12:1 that becoming a living sacrifice was an act of *worship.* The attitude of worship inspires giving of ourselves to a hurting humanity.

The apostles were careful not to let this become legalistic. They did not have an austere regulation of wealth where everyone looked the same, dressed the same, and possessed no individuality or privacy. It was simply a joyful community in which needs were met. It was not a case of the lazy being fed by the productive. It was simply willing hearts touching authentic needs.

How we are to make this aspect of the gospel practical is a part of the beauty of God at work in His people. It amazes me that leaders either feel threatened or are befuddled as how to touch their community. They can simply release their congregation to do what is in their hearts to do! They need to keep it balanced. But first, we must have true revival that will undergird our effort to feed, clothe, and house the needy. All the colors of the rainbow must be operative. The gospel must be preached so the world won't see us as simply a social agency. We must advance displaying the variety of God's character to humanity, but keeping in the forefront these good works which are a prominent part of continuous revival.

I suspect that the primary reason that God insists on

His children being generous is that the very confession "I am a child of God" means "I believe I am plugged into an unlimited source. It means that any material thing I possess can be replaced." Therefore, hoarding anything from the poor looks especially evil in a child of God because it is so unnecessary.

PRAYER: Prayer is the breath of true awakening. In this stage of revival, it takes on an even greater importance. Now that awakening has come, prayer, which was so central to the winning of the war, becomes threatened by the false sense of accomplishment that comes right after victory. Prayer which was a birth pang that brought revival to critical mass, must now become continuous. Prayer must focus on the need to keep the awakening balanced. We must pray for discernment so that Satan gains no subtle entrance. We must increase prayer for our leaders who are swimming in new waters and still finding their way. We must pray for the mass of new converts for their faith to grow, and contend for their safety.

Most importantly, however, the reason for continuous prayer is that the miracle of prayer must be passed on by example. First impressions are lasting, and going into an awakening, young believers should see us praying and praying always. Reproducing prayer warriors is the ultimate task. The apostles were so wise in implementing these three continuous acts: the pursuit of sanctification, service to the needy, and prayer. If only the church would realize the momentum of blessing these three acts in concert create!

Now we come to the last three features of the seventh stage of revival. They are the results of pleasing

God. The church has a proper attitude; caring and growing are in progress. Prayer is continuous, so now God has released His blessings. These are the kinds of blessings that Proverbs says will add no sorrow. God adds visibility, favor, and growth.

VISIBILITY: This feature is one in which the church becomes a light. God alerts the community to the presence of His people and opens their hearts to understand the true meaning of the gospel. More exactly, this feature is visible communication. Modern evangelism has been crippled by the most basic of problems. Secular society doesn't understand what we are saying. The ignition of the gospel's power is caused by precision in speaking God's heart. Only rarely does the church shed its tendency to add a side issue of filler to the message of life. Either we add human requirements or we dilute the rightful demands of Jesus. The result is that the Spirit of God cannot bring hearers to true conviction or true comfort. Paul describes this specifically in II Corinthians 4:1–6:

v. 1 Therefore, since through God's mercy we have his ministry, we do not lose heart.

v. 2 Rather, we have renounced secret and shameful ways; we do not use deception, nor do we distort the word of God. On the contrary, by setting forth the truth plainly we commend ourselves to every man's conscience in the sight of God.

v. 3 And even if our gospel is veiled, it is veiled to those who are perishing.

v. 4 The god of this age has blinded the minds of unbelievers, so that they cannot see the light of the gospel of the glory of Christ, who is the image of God.

v. 5 For we do not preach ourselves, but Jesus Christ as Lord, and ourselves as your servants for Jesus' sake.

v. 6 For God, who said, "Let light shine out of darkness," made his light shine in our hearts to give us the light of the knowledge of the glory of God in the face of Christ.

The core of believers in Acts 2 met daily in the temple courts and the word of their daily meetings spread to the entire city of Jerusalem. The news was spread by the Spirit of God. The Holy Spirit saw that this family of believers could be trusted, so He made them a candle— in essence, light—to a dark groping community.

This, I believe, is what is meant in the book of Revelation by the candlesticks representing the seven churches. Each had a lighthouse ability. They drew many to Christ; they were made visible. However, God warned them that their candlestick could be removed.

I have witnessed the rapid growth of churches that have been candlestick churches in our time. In many cases, the growth is so spectacular that local and national attention is drawn to the pastor and the congregation. I have also watched in dismay as some of these pastors have begun to attribute their phenomenal growth to human techniques that were obvious spiritual principles rewrapped in mystical language so as to sound new and revolutionary, drawing attention to the teacher. After this pattern of abuse has continued, and repeated warnings by the Holy Spirit have been ignored, suddenly the light from the candlestick has gone out. The results can be immediate. The church loses its magnetic personality. A once-powerful center of activity now becomes a hollow shell, a shadow of former glory.

Promotion of God's work is a very simple task for God. The only thing our Master needs is confidence in a congregation's motive. Soon word of our presence will spread through an entire community. The Holy Spirit himself will plead our cause "in the marketplace."

FAVOR: Proverbs 16:7 says, "When a man's ways please God, he makes even his enemies to be at peace with him."

Jesus was described as growing in stature and in favor with God and man (see Luke 2:52). Favor is an amazing blessing from God. By its power, Joseph rose from a prison cell to become prime minister of Egypt. Favor elevated Daniel from an exile to chief advisor of the king of Babylon. Resources to rebuild a city from ruins were released by this wondrous gift; Nehemiah knew God had pulled the heartstring of yet another king.

Jesus wants to open doors to your city. He can move the heart of a mayor to act on your behalf. God can give an entire city a marvelous bias toward His people. In Acts 2:47 we see that the believers were ". . . enjoying the favor of all the people." We can receive that same ability to influence for good. God can put in a good word for us. Once again, as God witnesses the purity of our motives, He grants favor. When God can rest in the assurance that we are bound to advance the kingdom of Christ, He will release whatever influence we need to do the job.

ADDED SOULS: "And the Lord added to their number daily those who were being saved." (Acts 2:47) Can anything reveal the health of a church more clearly than its desire for souls? At once I can detect the stench of an ingrown congregation or the vibrant fragrance of recent births. Added souls are the life of the church and something is desperately wrong with fellowships that can live without them.

America has experienced growth in the size of congregations, but tragically this growth is not so much from added souls as from transferred saints. Little churches have emptied into big ones and instead of having community impact, we have commuter congregations. People wander from church to church in search of that elusive spiritual mutation, "How to get blessed without commitment." The book of Acts army took a stand, captured a neighborhood, and converted it to God. We have surrendered to the enemy the moment we change directives. If the modern church replaces a strategy to conquer evil in a regional area with a program to attract the "restless already saved," we have lost the war and failed to be the church of Jesus Christ.

Frankly, God won't give souls to people who don't want them and who don't make room for them. He will not bless us with souls until we see that they are the greatest of blessings.

Let us sum up this seventh stage of revival. There are nine features. The first three pertain to attitude: devotion, expectancy, and worship, The next three are acts that come from these attitudes: training (sanctification), service to other believers and the world, and continuous prayer. Finally, the last three, which are responses to these attitudes and acts: visibility, favor, and souls.

Our entire goal is to reach critical mass and once the steel punch of God is felt, to move on to the greatest healing agency on earth: the Body of Christ operating in a healthy manner and on a daily basis.

This book is finished, but the campaign to bring America to God is just beginning. A radical departure from the norm is righteously called for. Until lightning strikes your heart and you long to make these truths come alive, this book, to you, is merely a block of paper. But if you are willing, I invite you to struggle and triumph with me as we follow after Christ in this, the church's finest hour.

Welcome to the war.

For other books, teaching cassettes and videos by **Mario Murillo**, write to:

Fresh Fire Communications
425 El Pintado Road
Danville, CA 94526
E-Mail: mario@mariomurilloministries.org